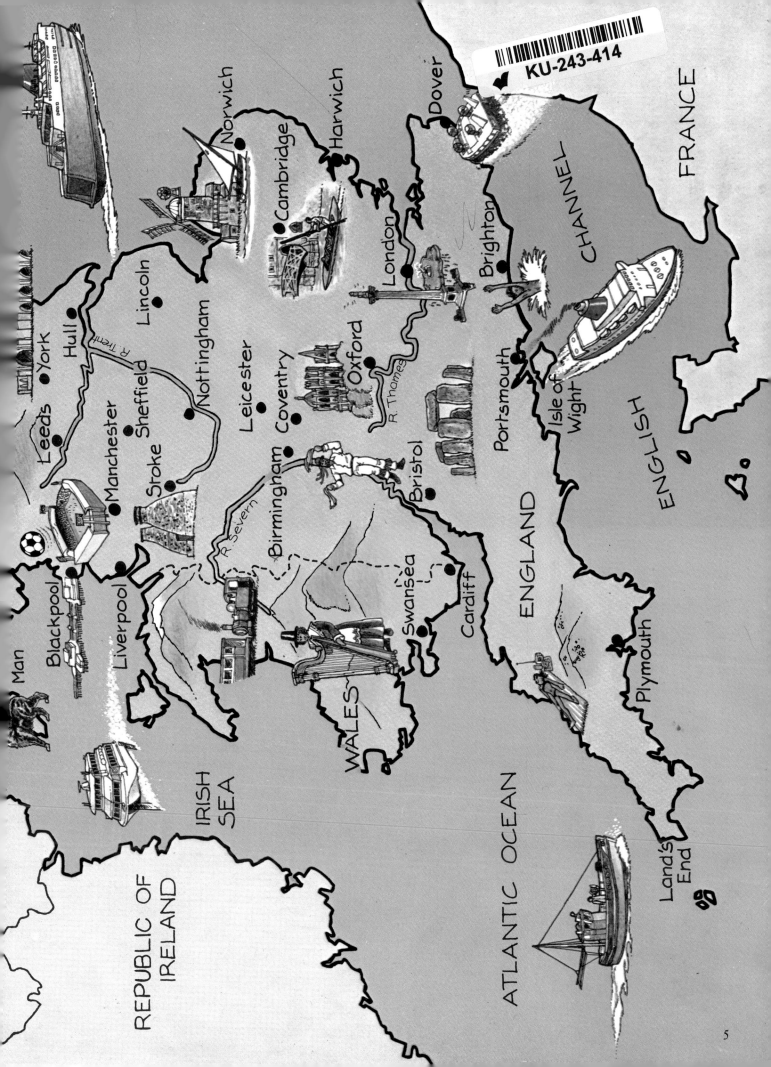

FRANCE

ENGLISH CHANNEL

Dover

Harwich

Norwich

Cambridge

London

Brighton

Lincoln

Nottingham

Oxford

R. Thames

Portsmouth

Isle of Wight

Hull

York

Leeds

R. Trent

Sheffield

Leicester

Coventry

Birmingham

Bristol

ENGLAND

Manchester

Stoke

R. Severn

Swansea

Cardiff

WALES

Blackpool

Liverpool

Man

IRISH SEA

Plymouth

ATLANTIC OCEAN

Land's End

REPUBLIC OF IRELAND

Contents

Great Britain is packed with a jumble of different-looking people. That is because their ancestors came from all over the world. About two thousand years ago the Romans invaded the island where Celtic tribes were living. After the Romans, came invasions of Saxons, Vikings, Normans and other European peoples. The invasions stopped long ago, but ever since, people from countries all over the world have come to live and settle here.

Great Britain is made up of three countries: England, Scotland and Wales. Many Scots and Welsh people speak their own languages. Even English words and sounds change from area to area. From ancient villages to modern cities, from wild mountains to peaceful flat plains, let's look at the fascinating mixture that is Great Britain!

This man is picking hops. Hops used to be picked by hand, but today there are machines to help in the harvesting.

The South East

The first sight of Great Britain for many visitors from Europe is the white chalk cliffs of Dover. Between the cliffs lies the busy harbour. Ferry boats and hovercraft come and go bringing goods and passengers to and from France and Belgium. High above the cliff-top stands Dover Castle. The Romans built a lighthouse on top of these cliffs when they first came to Britain. Since then, for two thousand years, there has always been a fort above the harbour.

Nearby is the entrance to a Channel Tunnel.

People have dreamed for many years of making a tunnel to connect Britain and France, but so far the entrance is all that has been built. One day you will probably drive a car, or ride in a train, under the Channel. You might even cross *over* it; some people think a bridge is a better idea.

Dover is in Kent, the county which is known as 'The Garden of England'. Apples and hops are Kent's most famous crops. Some of the apples are used to make delicious cider. Hops are used in making beer. Just as French and Spanish people are proud of their wines, so the British are proud of their beers.

In September the hops are ready for picking. Not so long ago, this was a holiday pastime for poor London families. Parents and children worked together in the hop gardens, cutting down the strings and picking the hops off the vines. When the hard work was over, they had a great outdoor party, called the Hop Festival. After the festival, they returned to London, the capital city of Great Britain.

A cross-Channel hovercraft. Hovercrafts are supported above the water by a cushion of air. Even so, if you ride in one you might think you were being driven down a bumpy road.

London

Every weekday morning, central London's streets are jammed with people who have come by bus, car or train from the edges of the city to work in the banks, offices and shops. Some of the men still wear black jackets, bowler hats and grey striped trousers, which used to be the uniform of the 'City' workers.

The City of London, or 'the City', is the site of the original Roman town. Crowded with offices and buildings, it covers just one square mile (256 hectares). When we talk of London today, we mean a huge city, one of the world's largest. But really, it is made up of many small towns and villages joined together around the old city.

A Pearly King jokes with a Pearly girl.

The ravens that live in the grounds of the Tower of London are very carefully guarded. Legend has it that if the ravens leave, the Tower will fall down.

Stacked high with goods for London, these sailing barges crowded the River Thames in the last century. Today big steamers carry the goods and they rarely come as far up the river as London. People have lovingly restored these old barges. Once a year they are raced on the Thames.

One village which is now part of London is Lambeth, on the south side of the River Thames. Lambeth's most famous inhabitants are the Pearlies, sometimes called Pearly Kings and Queens. They take their name from the hundreds of pearl buttons that they sew all over their clothes. You might see some of them at fairs collecting money for good causes.

Some people call all Londoners 'Cockneys', but that is not really correct. To be a true Cockney, you must have been born within the sound of the bells of Bow Church, to the east of the City.

The most famous of all the bridges over the River Thames is London Bridge, which leads into the City itself. The present bridge is a new one, the third in fact. The first London Bridge was covered with houses and shops from bank to bank. There are many stories about Old London Bridge, but perhaps the strangest is the tale of the Pedlar of Swaffham.

The Pedlar of Swaffham

Once, long ago in the little market town of Swaffham in Norfolk, there lived a pedlar called John Chapman. He was a hard-working man. With his pack on his back and his dog at his heels, he walked from village to village for miles around. He sold all sorts of things, cotton thread and needles, knick-knacks and spices, to the housewives at their doors.

One day, as he slept by the road, John had a dream. In his dream he was told that if he went to London Bridge and stood there for three days, he would hear some very good news. At first he ignored the dream, but he dreamed it again that night and again the night after that. The next morning he decided to set off for London.

In those days the only way for a poor man to get about the country was to walk, so John walked to London, with his pack on his back and his dog at his heels. It took him three days and three nights. When he arrived he was so tired that he fell asleep on the bridge outside a butcher's shop.

When morning came, he rose to his feet, rubbed his sore back and set out his wares on the ground. Amongst the needles, cotton and spices, he waited to hear the good news.

For three whole days he stood on the bridge, but no one bought anything from him and no one spoke to him at all. At the end of the third day the butcher came out of his shop. 'Good evening, my friend,' said the butcher. 'I've watched you standing there for three days, and I don't believe you've sold a thing. You look like a country chap: what brings you to the big city?'

John told him of his dream and of the long journey he had made, but he didn't tell him where he had come from. No one in London had ever heard of Swaffham anyway. When John had finished, the butcher howled with laughter.

'You must be more of a fool than you look, my country friend, to believe such a silly dream. Why, I had a dream myself last night. I was told that if I went to some little town I've never even heard of, called Swaffham or something like that, I would find a pot of gold buried under a tree in a pedlar's garden. I don't know where the town is, but even if I did, I'm not such a fool as to make such a long journey just because of a dream.'

John laughed too and pretended to be sorry for his foolishness. 'I'm sure you're right, Master Butcher,' he said. 'I had better go back to my home and not waste my time on such foolish errands.' But inside he was bursting with excitement. His dream was coming true. As quickly as he could, he gathered up his wares and set off back to Norfolk, with his pack on his back and his dog at his heels.

When he got home he dug a great hole in his garden, under the tree. Before long, he uncovered a pot. On the lid was some writing in Latin which John could not understand. But no matter, for inside the pot was the treasure, gold coins to make him rich.

One day a travelling priest came to Swaffham, so John asked him what the words on the lid meant. The priest read them and told him: 'Under me there lies another far greater than I.' When John heard this he ran out to his garden and at the bottom of the hole he dug down again. Eventually, he found another pot of gold, twice as big as the first.

He used the money to open a school in Swaffham and to pay for the rebuilding of the church. When he died the people of the town raised a statue to him in the market place. He can be seen there to this day, with his pack on his back and his dog at his heels. So you see dreams can come true, but not always as you might expect.

East Anglia

Punting at Cambridge. The town has one of England's two oldest universities; the other is in Oxford.

You can still walk along the road the pedlar used for the first part of his walk to London. Most of it is still a wide footpath, just as he would remember it. It is called the Peddar's Way ('peddar' is an old way of spelling pedlar). It was used by the Romans and probably by Stone Age travellers before them. It crosses half of Norfolk, passing close to Swaffham.

The counties of Norfolk, Suffolk and part of Cambridgeshire are known as East Anglia. East Anglia is good farming country, especially in the west, where small villages slumber among gentle hills. Many village houses are thatched, their roofs covered with reeds laid and tied cleverly on a criss-cross wooden frame. The roofs may look old-fashioned, but inside they are warm and dry.

The reeds grow on the edges of the flat land around the Norfolk Broads, a large network of pools and streams. Once the Broads were dry land, but long ago the peat that lay under the

The Broads are a very popular place for boating holidays. So many boats use the waterways that a speed limit is needed.

Thatching is a very skilled job. The best thatchers, and the best reeds, come from Norfolk.

soil was dug out for fuel. About six hundred years ago the peat-diggings were flooded by the sea. Ever since they have stayed flooded.

The same storm might have covered a Saxon village, West Stow, in a sand drift. It lay hidden by sand for hundreds of years until some builders uncovered it. Now it is partly rebuilt, you can see what a Saxon village looked like.

In the south of East Anglia is Cambridge. Behind its ancient university colleges is a network of canals called the Backs. In the summer a favourite student pastime is to go up and down the Backs in punts, long flat-bottomed boats which are pushed along with a pole.

A leaping Morris dancer.

Bristol and the Cotswolds

Bristol

Six or eight men, of all ages, dressed in white shirts and trousers, form up in two lines. They have bright cross-belts on their chests and leather patches below their knees. They hold handkerchiefs or sticks in their hands. In front of them, a musician plays a fiddle or a concertina. They begin to dance, jumping and stamping in time to the music to make the bells on their leather patches jingle.

This is a very old form of dancing called Morris Dancing. Although it can be seen all over England, it is most common in the Cotswold Hills, among the old stone villages and rolling farmland of this beautiful part of England.

The villages are built of Cotswold Stone, which was dug from nearby quarries. It is a golden colour, like honey, and it is easy to split. Even the roofs of the houses are made of stone tiles. The tiles are often covered in moss or even grass on the oldest houses.

This is sheep-farming country and the wool trade has been important here for hundreds of years. The wool cut from a sheep is called a fleece. Public houses in the area are often called 'The Fleece' or 'The Packhorse' and will have painted signs showing how the bales of wool used to be carried about on horseback.

Many of the bales were carried to Bristol, the great sea-port of the west. Now the big ships stop outside the city, at the mouth of the River Avon, but not long ago they came right into town.

In Bristol you can see an old ship called the

Great Britain. When she was built in 1843, she was the world's first large propeller-driven steam ship. After many years of hard work, disaster struck her. In 1886 she was caught in a hurricane near the tip of South America and was forced to shelter on a lonely beach in the Falkland Islands. She lay rotting there until 1970 when she was towed back 12,000 km to the same Bristol dock where she was built all those years ago. Now a group of people are busy restoring her to her original appearance. One day, when all the work is finished, you will be able to stand on her decks and admire the splendid iron ship that once took passengers in luxury to America and Australia.

Today some rich people fly to America in *Concorde.* Close to Bristol there is a huge factory where the supersonic aircraft was built. *Concorde* was so expensive that the French and English had to get together to build it.

If you go to Bristol by train, you may be whisked down on a High Speed Train at 200 km per hour. High above, flies Concorde.

Great Britain *arrives home again. Isambard Kingdom Brunel, the man who designed her, also built the graceful Clifton suspension bridge that can be seen in the background.*

Play shove ha'penny!

A favourite meeting place is the public house, or pub, where adults can gather in the evenings to enjoy a drink with their friends. All pubs have names. Most have brightly painted signs outside, illustrating the name.

Some are named after kings of England or famous historical characters, like 'The George' or 'The Nelson'. Others might show the sign of a plough or a bull, in farming country. A very common name is 'The Royal Oak', in memory of the time when King Charles II escaped from his enemies by hiding in an oak tree. See how many signs you can spot if you travel round the country.

British people love to play games and there are several games associated with pubs, such as darts, dominoes and skittles. One game which used to be played by the king and his friends, but which is now found in pubs instead of palaces, is called Shove Ha'penny. It is a game of great skill and it has been played in Britain for hundreds of years. Here is how to make your own shove ha'penny board and play with your friends.

In Celtic times, or even earlier, people held May festivals when they would crown a May Queen. Her 'subjects' included Jack-in-the-Green, who was supposed to represent Spring. His name lives on in one of the most common pub names, the Green Man. Inside the pub you can just see someone playing darts.

To Play: *Each player takes it in turn to 'hit' five coins. The first person to get three coins in each 'bed' is the winner. (A bed is the space between two lines.) At the end of five hits, the player makes a mark by the side of each coin in a bed. A coin is only in bed if it does not touch the lines! During your five hits, you can hit one coin to push* *another. When you have three marks by a bed it is full and you cannot score again by that bed. If you leave a coin in a full bed, the other player gets the point. If a coin does not reach the front line, you may have it again. Coins hit over the back line are 'dead' and can not be used until the next player's turn.*

You will need

3 35mm long screws

screwdriver

hole punch

ball-point pen

a piece of 20mm thick blockboard 350 × 550mm (ask for an off-cut, it will be cheaper)

coins (about 25mm across)

thin piece of balsa wood 350 × 70mm

drawing pins

piece of wood 20 × 20 × 350mm

fine sandpaper

wood polish

rag

1. Smooth edges and both sides of board with block and sand paper. Blow dust away.

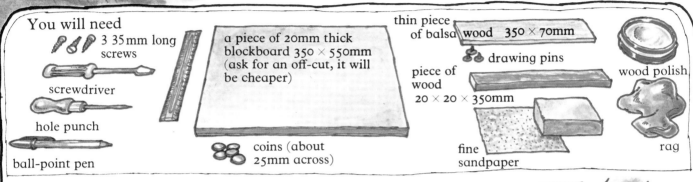

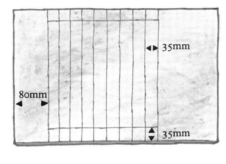

2. Using a ruler and biro, draw a line 80 mm from the short end and then nine more lines 35 mm apart. Measure in 35 mm from both the long sides and draw two lines running at right angles to the nine lines.

3. Apply polish over the board and use a cloth to polish it up. Repeat at least once. The more you polish your board, the faster the coins will fly!

4. Make three holes with the hole punch in the strip of wood. Turn the board over and screw the strip at the front end of the board.

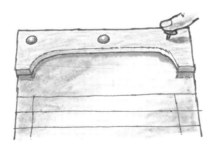

5. Turn the board over and pin the piece of balsa wood along the top end with drawing pins. This will catch the stray coins.

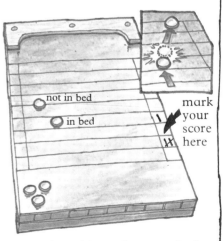

not in bed

in bed

mark your score here

6. Your board is ready now. At the top of the page are the rules.

Devon and Cornwall

Two great British heroes came from the West Country, which is the name given to the counties of Devon and Cornwall. Sir Francis Drake was one of these heroes. He came from Plymouth, in Devon, where the men have always been famous as skilful sailors. In 1588 he bravely led a navy of tiny ships which drove off the huge ships of the Spanish Armada when they tried to invade England. Plymouth Harbour is still used today by ships of the Royal Navy.

Scottish fishermen at a Cornish harbour unloading their catch onto lorries bound for the big London markets. All over Britain fishermen are having to sail further and further away to find fish. The fish supply in the seas around Great Britain is running out because so many boats have fished there.

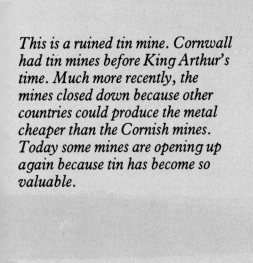

This is a ruined tin mine. Cornwall had tin mines before King Arthur's time. Much more recently, the mines closed down because other countries could produce the metal cheaper than the Cornish mines. Today some mines are opening up again because tin has become so valuable.

The other great hero is King Arthur. Although we are not sure if he was a real person, many people believe he really *did* exist and that he was born in Cornwall about 1,400 years ago. He was probably a British chieftain who led the British against the invading Saxons. All kinds of tales have been told about him and his band of men, the Knights of the Round Table and his magician, Merlin. There is a fine Cornish castle at Tintagel, which is said to be the site of Arthur's castle. The ruins you can explore now are the remains of a later castle.

In St Austell the main industry is China clay mining. The scenery in a claypit is astonishing. Huge snow-white hills rise up around bright green pools. The streams around them run white, like milk. The streams are white because the clay is washed out of the pit sides with powerful water hoses. The hills are the rock dust, which is what is left behind after the clay has been removed. China clay was originally used to make fine china – cups, saucers and plates. Today it is used in making other things as well, such as paint, toothpaste and paper.

The Midlands

When china was first made in Britain, the clay to make it was very expensive because it came all the way from China. That is why it is called China clay. One of the first men to use the China clay found in England was Josiah Wedgwood. He opened a huge pottery works in Staffordshire in 1769. Even before then, part of the Midlands was called the Potteries because so many potters worked there.

Staffordshire china is famous all over the world for its graceful shapes and fine decoration. When it is first fired, or baked, pottery is called 'biscuit ware', because it is rough and looks dull.

Once clay was fired in these bottle kilns. Some are still standing, but most clay is now fired by electricity. Once, hundreds of these kilns with their stubby chimneys filled the air around the Potteries with choking black smoke.

As well as delicate china, lots of other things are made in the Potteries. These are Toby jugs. Sometimes they are painted to look like famous people.

Later colours and shiny glaze are added and it is fired again, sometimes twice, to become china.

The potters used to have difficulty transporting their products around the country. On bumpy roads, the china could be broken before anyone had a chance to use it. One answer was the canal. About the same time that Wedgwood opened his pottery works, people began building canals all over Britain to carry coal, wood, iron and also pottery. Now the pottery and china could be carried as smoothly as anyone could wish.

Railways and roads now do most of the work the canals used to do, but some pottery still goes to London in long barges called 'narrow boats'.

The biggest industry in the Midlands is making cars, but there are other smaller trades too. Redditch, near Birmingham, is well-known for its needles. Nottingham is famous throughout the world for its lace and bicycles. Birmingham itself has so many small businesses that it is called the 'City of a Thousand Trades'.

Let us see how all this began.

When the railways were built people gradually stopped using the canals. Nowadays canals are mainly used for peaceful boating holidays. You can see one of the old narrow boats and its horse which pulls it along the canal.

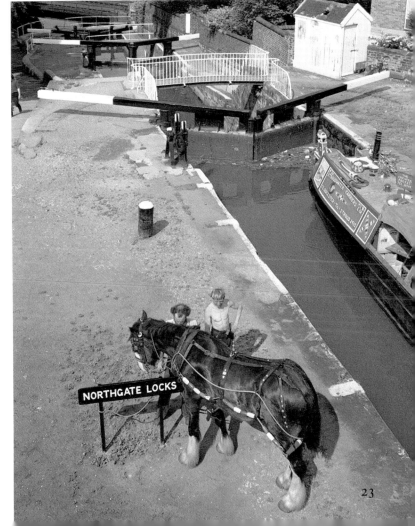

NORTHGATE LOCKS

A revolution

Machines to spin wool; machines to weave cloth; machines to cut and smooth wood; machines to stitch shoes. There was a time when new machines seemed to be appearing every day. Before they were invented all these trades were done by hand. To the people who first used them, the machines must have seemed like magic, though to us they look old-fashioned.

The time when the machines were being invented, about two hundred and fifty years ago, is called the Industrial Revolution. Changes happened so quickly and affected so many peoples' lives that it really did seem like a revolution. It all started in Britain. Later, other countries took up the new ideas. Many of the machines in Britain have been looked after in memory of the brilliant engineers who invented them.

There is an open-air museum at Ironbridge, in Shropshire, where a collection of enormous steam-engines reminds us of these old days. The village is named after the iron bridge that crosses the River Severn there. It was the first iron bridge in the world.

At Sticklepath, in Devon, there is an old mill driven by a waterwheel. The water comes from a nearby stream in wooden channels. A wooden gate is opened and the water falls on to the paddles of the wheel. It falls with such power that the wheel turns with a sound like thunder.

Inside the mill there are machines that are driven by the power of the water wheel. All the machinery works. Since the mill is now a museum, you can watch the machines that once hammered iron into scythes, ploughshares and other farm tools.

The factories which were built in the areas where wool was produced were also called mills. At first they worked by water-power, but later by steam power. Many of these old mills can be seen in Yorkshire. You can also see the small towns which grew up around wool mills. When

On the left is a preserved steam railway. It is fascinating to see the trains working the way they used to, but really most people work the railway just for fun! Many children help at weekends doing odd jobs. Perhaps they are dreaming that one day they will be able to drive a steam engine.

the factories arrived, country people had to give up using their slow hand looms. They had to move to work in the factories instead and live in the new towns.

There are remains of early industry all over Britain. But when you take a train, you are travelling on the one thing that was most important to the Industrial Revolution, the railways.

This is the iron bridge that gave Iron Bridge its name. It is hard to imagine, but once this peaceful countryside echoed to the clash of machines and the blast of furnaces as the early factories made iron to make the machines of the Industrial Revolution.

Build the railway!

The first railways were built by tough hardworking men called 'navvies'. They got their name from the 'navigators' – the men who had built the canals just before the railways. Railways were much faster than canals and soon railway lines were being built all over the country. But not everybody wanted the railways. Farmers thought the engines would scare their animals; canal owners knew they would lose business. The first engines were not very powerful, so the lines had to be as flat as possible. When you play this game, you will see some of the problems the early railway builders faced.

How to play: *you will need a dice and some counters. Each player throws the dice and the person who throws the highest number starts. Then each player throws in turn, following the instructions you will find on the way. When you reach the red square, you must decide whether to take the left or right route, but remember, the short route may not be the quickest! The first person to build the line to Seaport wins.*

The weather is uncertain, throw dice again. Go back if it is an odd number, go forward if even.

Navvies work extra hard, go on 3 spaces.

Viaduct finished ahead of time, go on 3 spaces.

Navvies' food supply held up, go back 2 spaces.

Land is very flat, go on three spac[es]

Navvies in fight with local townspeople, miss a go.

Lord Muck will not let you build on his land, take the purple route.

Navvies have cholera, go back 4 spaces.

Weather is fine; have another go.

Owner of coal mine gives you more money to help build railway, have another go.

Start

Coaltown

26

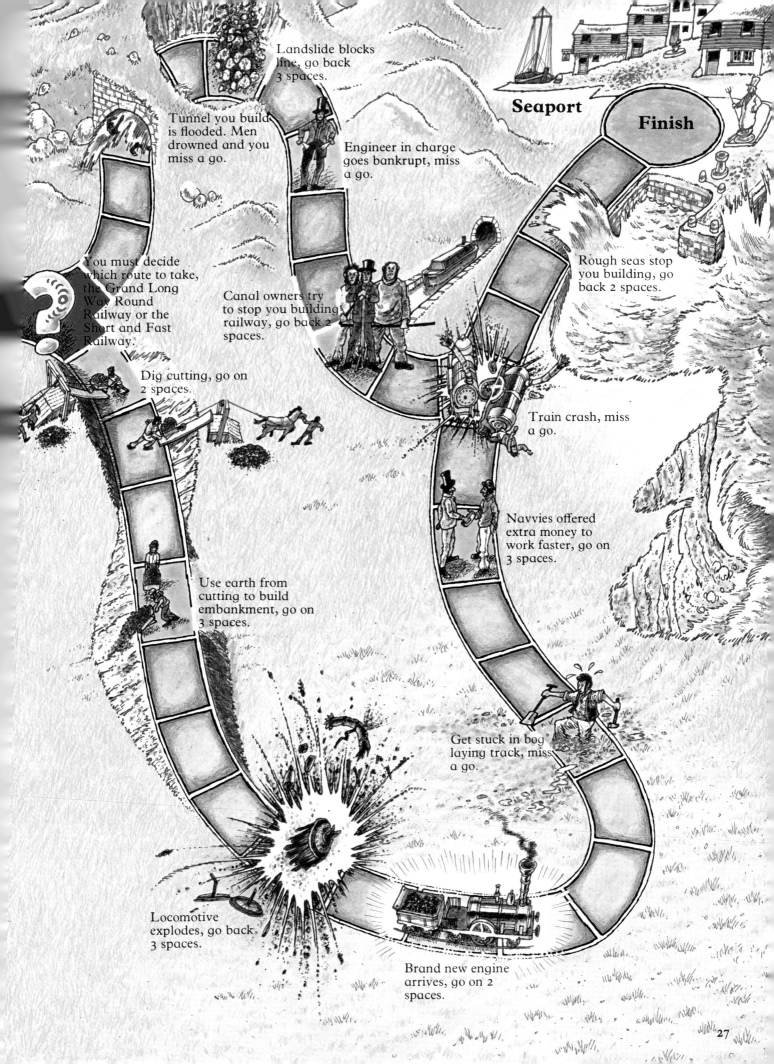

Seaport

Finish

Landslide blocks line, go back 3 spaces.

Tunnel you build is flooded. Men drowned and you miss a go.

Engineer in charge goes bankrupt, miss a go.

You must decide which route to take, the Grand Long Way Round Railway or the Short and Fast Railway.

Canal owners try to stop you building railway, go back 2 spaces.

Rough seas stop you building, go back 2 spaces.

Dig cutting, go on 2 spaces.

Train crash, miss a go.

Navvies offered extra money to work faster, go on 3 spaces.

Use earth from cutting to build embankment, go on 3 spaces.

Get stuck in bog laying track, miss a go.

Locomotive explodes, go back 3 spaces.

Brand new engine arrives, go on 2 spaces.

Yorkshire and the North East

The first industries to be changed by the Industrial Revolution were spinning and weaving. They grew up in the north of England, where wool was plentiful growing on the backs of flocks of sheep in the Yorkshire Dales. Cotton came from North America. The towns that were built among the sheep pastures are now great cities. In Yorkshire, the cities of Bradford, Huddersfield and Leeds are now huge. They are joined by motorways

Hebden Bridge, below, is near Leeds. This old mill town clings to the moor valley. In Yorkshire these valleys are called dales.

The boys above are pretending to attack the Roman soldiers defending the ruins of Hadrian's Wall. The Romans built the wall to keep the wild Scottish tribes out of Roman England.

into one gigantic industrial area. The woollen cloth that is made here is still world-famous.

The Pennine Hills stretch along the middle of England between the two industrial areas to the east and west. They are a favourite place for walking, away from the bustle of the cities, high up in the open air.

Families go out at weekends to walk on the Pennines in some of the most beautiful scenery in Britain. Walking there is a joy but it needs to be taken seriously. The hills can be wild and stormy. You should wear proper boots and clothing.

The Pennines reach up through Yorkshire and County Durham to the Scottish borders. Once a year, Durham City is the scene of a splendid parade called the Miners' Gala. It was started to celebrate the time when trade unions were made legal. Each year members of every trade in Britain come to join in. It is like an enormous party with flags and banners, brass or silver bands and all the fun of the fair.

Many people in Newcastle and along the coast work at coal-mining, engineering or fishing. The North Sea coast here is beautiful, but wild. For the people who have to sail the North Sea it is very dangerous and there have been many wrecks. Sailors' graves fill local churchyards.

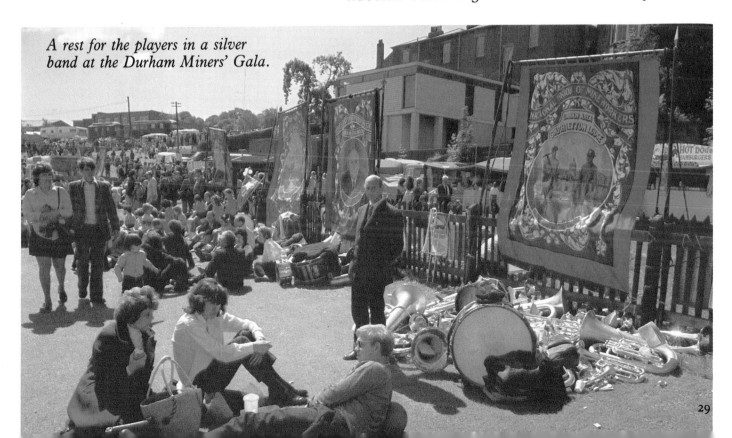

A rest for the players in a silver band at the Durham Miners' Gala.

Grace Darling, heroine of the North Sea

In the north east, off the Northumberland coast, the summer sun glints brightly off the blue North Sea. You might never imagine that in winter this place can be deadly dangerous. Gales sweeping down from the North Sea hurl waves ten metres and more – higher than a house – into the air. Spray from the waves drifts across the cliffs like smoke amongst the crashing breakers. That is the time when all sailors wish they were safely at home and not risking their lives out on the cruel sea.

There are lighthouses along the coast to warn sailors of the most dangerous rocks. In one of those lighthouses, the Longstone Light, near the Farne Islands, lived a lighthouse keeper, William Darling, with his daughter, Grace. It was 1838. In those days the keepers were allowed to live with their families in the lighthouses. Nowadays,

the men must work alone, but for twelve people that year it was a blessing that the girl was there by her father's side.

On the night of September 6, a fearful storm blew up along the coast. Grace and her father watched the furious sea from the safety and warmth of their stone lighthouse. They pitied any poor sailors out there.

Suddenly, through the swirling mists, they saw flickering lights. It was the steamer *Forfarshire*, making her regular voyage from Hull to Dundee, in Scotland. Grace shook her father's arm.

'Look,' she cried, 'that ship's trying to get between the island and the mainland.'

'Yes,' replied her father. 'She must have engine trouble. Any ship with sound engines would keep well away from the shore on a night like this.'

He was right. In fact, the ship's engines had failed. In desperation, the captain hoisted sail as he tried to make for calmer water between the island and shore. It was hopeless. The ship was at the mercy of the storm and, helplessly, she drifted out of control. With a dreadful crash and the sound of tearing wood, the ship was slammed onto the rocks. The huge waves began to pound her to pieces. Most of the passengers and crew were drowned almost immediately.

Grace and her father watched in horror, convinced that nobody could survive the wreck. Then Grace saw an amazing sight. A man had struggled from the wreck up onto the rocks and was frantically waving. As she watched, the man was joined by more scrambling figures. Eventually, she could see twelve people clinging to the rocks.

'Nobody could get to those poor souls in this weather,' sighed William. 'They'll be lost for sure. If *only* we could help.'

'But Father, we must!' cried Grace. 'We've got a boat and I'm strong. I'll row with you to rescue them. Together, we can get them off the rocks and back to safety.'

William Darling's boat was only seven metres long, an open fishing boat. Grace and her father struggled to launch it out into the angry sea and began rowing towards the rocks. The distance was less than a kilometre, but it took the pair of them half an hour to get there. They were exhausted when they arrived, but there was no time to lose. Grace held the boat steady while her father clambered out to help the survivors into the boat. They battled back with six people on that first trip, including a mother and her two children. When they reached the safety of the lighthouse, Grace looked after four of the survivors while her father started back to the wreck, helped by two of the rescued men. In the morning, when the survivors had rested a little, William rowed them back to the mainland.

Grace was twenty-two years old and the story of her bravery spread around the country like wildfire. Grace Darling was famous throughout the whole of Britain as the heroine of Longstone Light.

I do like to be beside the seaside

Blackpool and the Lakes

A shepherd and his dog at a sheep dog trial. The shepherd 'speaks' to his dog with a series of different whistles. Each whistle tells the dog what to do.

Blackpool

The lonely Northumberland coast is very different from the Lancashire coast on the other side of England. Here you can walk along the road with the sea on one side and a town on the other. There are long beaches to play on and swim from. Shellfish, such as whelks and cockles, are sold from street stalls. Or would you prefer a peppermint rock stick with the town's name running through it?

Blackpool beach on a summer's day is not the place for peace and quiet! In the background is Blackpool's pier. You can see similar piers at other seaside towns but some of them are over a hundred years old and are falling down.

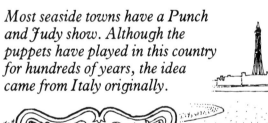

Most seaside towns have a Punch and Judy show. Although the puppets have played in this country for hundreds of years, the idea came from Italy originally.

The town's name is Blackpool, the most famous seaside town in Britain. Crowds of people go there from the cities to have a week or two of fun. You can walk to the end of the pier, where, if you like, you can sit and fish. Then there is the famous Tower. You do not need a map to find it – it is over 170 m high and can be seen from far away. If all that is not enough, you can visit a circus, an aquarium or a zoo. On autumn nights the long sea front road, the promenade, is lit up like an electric firework display.

Just north of this busy holiday town is one of the most peaceful parts of Britain, the Lake District. Mountains, streams, lakes and high rocks make this a favourite place for a walking holiday amongst beautiful scenery. People come here to climb England's highest mountain, Scafell Pike, which is 980 m high.

In summer sheepdog trials are held here. Shepherds with carefully trained dogs see which dog is best at rounding up sheep from the hills. Some of the best sheepdogs come from Wales.

Wales

A higher mountain than any in England is Snowdon, in North Wales. It rises 1,095 m above sea level. Its Welsh name is Eryri, which means 'Eagle Top'. At the top, you feel like an eagle flying high above the country below.

There are several ways of reaching the top of Snowdon, depending on how energetic you feel. You can use the mountain railway, ride up on a pony or just walk. Lots of people go up by train and then walk down.

If you walk on the mountain, you must be very careful. Mists can cover the slopes very quickly. People who have got lost have had bad accidents. Mountain guides will help walkers; if a mist falls, the best thing to do is to sit still and wait for the guide to find you.

Near Snowdon, in the coastal town of Caernarvon, is a fine castle with a story to tell. For hundreds of years the English and the Welsh quarrelled over who should rule Wales, the Welsh or the English. In 1284 the English King Edward I stayed at Caernarvon when his son was born. A great ceremony was hold at which the King held up his son to the watching crowd. 'Here is your Prince', he told them. But the Welsh were not satisfied and the fighting did not stop until many years later. Ever since that first ceremony, the eldest son of the English monarch has had the title of Prince of Wales.

At the very north-western tip of Wales is the island of Anglesey. If you visit it, you will meet people who never speak English. Instead, they speak the ancient and beautiful Welsh language. People all over Wales speak Welsh, but on Anglesey it is the main language. A village on the

On the left, Prince Charles is crowned Prince of Wales at Caernarvon Castle in 1969. One day he will be King of England, Wales and Scotland.

This is Snowdonia. This mountainous area is named after its highest mountain, Snowdon. On a fine day the views from the mountain tops are worth the effort of climbing them.

island has the longest name in the world. Here it is: Llanfairpwllgwyngyllgogerychwyrndrob-wllllantysiliogogogoch. Many Welsh sounds are different from those in English and the name is spoken like this: 'Thlan fair poolth gwin gilth go gerri hooerndro boolth thlanti sillio go go goh'. Try saying that all in one! It means: 'The church of St Mary in the hollow of the white hazel near the swift whirlpool of Llantysilio of the red cave'. Local people call it Llanfair P.G. for short.

Not many people outside Wales understand Welsh, but the Welsh people are world-famous for two other things apart from their language – rugby football and music.

Welsh customs

Along the South Wales coast is a line of industrial cities. Behind these big cities, Swansea, Cardiff and Newport, deep valleys stretch up into the hills. Once, most men in the valleys worked in coal mines. But it cost more to dig out some of the coal than it could be sold for. Many mines closed and many people lost their jobs. Now oil is so expensive, it may be worth opening the mines again.

To relax from their hard work, Welsh people love playing music and games. Welsh choirs are the best in Britain and you will often hear them singing on radio or in concerts. As for games, the Welsh are champions at the game of rugby football.

The great stadium at Cardiff, called the Arms Park, is the headquarters of Welsh rugby, but perhaps it is better to see a game in one of the mining valleys. Around the pitch are mining machinery and coal dust tips. Behind them are

In ancient times, the Celts of Britain and France were led by priests called Druids. Today, the Druids meet to choose the best Welsh-speaking poet.

Almost nothing stops the Welsh playing rugby. The two opposing 'packs' strain against each other in a 'scrum', each side heaving for the ball. What with the roaring crowd, it seems more of a battle than a game.

magnificent green hills. Nearly all the town's people go to see their team play a rival team.

After the game comes the singing. Most songs are Welsh. Some are sad love songs, others are the same hymns that are sung in the small valley churches. Everyone sings; on a quiet night you can hear lovely singing drifting up the valley.

Every town is proud of its choir; people often join when they are children. Once a year many towns have an *Eisteddfod*. This is a competition to find the best singers and poets in the town. Naturally, most competitions are held in Welsh. The biggest competition is the International Eisteddfod in Llangollen in central Wales. Poets, dancers, musicians and singers come from all over the world for the festivities.

It may surprise you that people in Brittany, in northern France, are closely linked to the Welsh. Both are Celts and have similar languages; both delight in music and poetry. But closer to Wales than France is another country with ancient Celtic traditions – Scotland.

A Highland Gathering. This strong man is tossing the caber. He must try and make it turn end over end before it lands.

The Scottish Highlands

The Highlands of Scotland can be very lonely; the land is poor and very few people live there. Deep wooded valleys in the heather-covered hills are called glens. Often, at the end of a glen, stands a castle. Some castles are ruined, others are still lived in, but they all tell the same story, of battles long ago between rival clans.

A clan consisted of all the relations and followers of a chieftain, like a huge family. The clan battles stopped long ago, but Scottish people are still fiercely proud of the clans they belong to. Many Scottish surnames are old clan names such as Macdonald or Maclean.

Each clan had its own special tartan, a woollen material woven in a pattern of coloured squares, worn by all members of the clan. People still wear them today.

In the summer, clans meet to hold competitions for music, dancing and games.

If you travel along the road that runs beside Loch Ness, watch the water! You might see Nessie, which is what Scottish people call the mysterious monster.

A woman or girl wears her tartan as a long skirt, with a *plaid*, like a folded shawl, over one shoulder. Men and boys wear kilts and black velvet jackets with silver buttons. They carry purses, called *sporrans*, on straps around their waists.

Some of the sports at a Highland Gathering seem strange to a visitor. Putting-the-shot and tug-of-war are well-known at other athletic meetings, but other sports, such as caber tossing, are much less well known outside Scotland.

Music and dancing are the most exciting things at a Gathering. Scotland's national instrument, the bagpipes, is played in piping competitions. It is also played for the dancing contests. There are solo competitions for *flings* and *reels*, energetic dances with fast, complicated steps. Other dances are more gentle and graceful and men and women dance together.

Running through the Highlands is a gloomy deep valley called the Great Glen. In it there is a long, narrow and very deep lake called Loch Ness. Loch is the Scottish word for lake. For many years people told stories of a mysterious monster living in the lake, but only a few local people believed them. Recently, though, scientists with special underwater cameras have taken some pictures here that look as if they might be of a prehistoric animal. But the waters are very deep and dark and the pictures are fuzzy. Who knows? Perhaps there really *is* something very strange and exciting in Loch Ness.

Oil! Petrol, plastics, soap and even animal food – these are just a few things made from oil. East of the Scottish coast lie the stormy North Sea oil fields. This oil rig is being towed out to sea where it will become home for 70 men They lead a tough, hard life, helping to get the 'black gold' ashore.

The Scottish Lowlands

The southern part of Scotland is called the Lowlands, an area of gentle rolling hills and lochs, with small farms and villages. Scotland's two biggest cities, Edinburgh and Glasgow, are here. Most Scottish people live in or around the cities.

Glasgow is a big busy industrial city on the River Clyde. It has two rival football teams, Rangers and Celtic. Everybody in Glasgow supports one or the other. A match between them brings the city to a halt, when everyone goes to the ground or watches on television.

Edinburgh is very different. Each year it holds Britain's most important music and drama festival. People from all over the world take part. At the end of the festival, there is a floodlit tattoo at the castle. Soldiers parade in front of the castle to the eerie music of bagpipes and drums. Some people think bagpipe music is the most exciting there is. Others think it is the most awful sound in the world, like cats fighting. But hear it yourself and make up your own mind.

If you walk in Scotland, sooner or later you will pass a forest. As you get closer, you may hear an angry buzzing noise. That will be foresters using power saws to cut down the trees for timber. Hundreds of years ago over half of Scotland was covered by trees. But over the years many forests were cleared for timber or for farmland. Forests were even burnt down to kill off dangerous wolves. Nowadays foresters make sure there are always new trees to replace the ones that have been cut down.

Timber! On the left a forester trims the branches off the tree trunk before it is dragged away by a tractor.

Edinburgh castle overlooks the city. In front of it crowds watch the floodlit tattoo. Hundreds of years ago Scotland had its own monarch. In the castle are kept the ancient Scottish Crown Jewels.

In the far south-west, just near the border with England, is the tiny village of Gretna Green. In the village is a blacksmith's shop with a strange story. Scotland and England have different laws. Young English couples, whose parents would not let them marry, used to run away to Scotland to get married. Gretna Green was the nearest Scottish village for most English people and the blacksmith was allowed to conduct marriages. The laws are now changed, but people still like to get married at the shop in the old way.

Tea time!

Each area of Britain has its own special foods and Scotland is no exception. Scottish porridge, shortbread and oat cakes are eaten all over the world. You may have heard of haggis, too, but maybe you do not like the idea of eating a stuffed sheep-stomach (it is really very nice).

If you walk down a British street, you might think the British had stopped eating *British* food. You will see restaurants serving Indian, Chinese, Italian, Greek, French and even American food! But soon you will find a fish and chip shop. Every town has one and, long before you see it, you will smell delicious fried fish and potatoes.

But at home, roast beef is an old Sunday lunch favourite, eaten with crisp Yorkshire Pudding and fresh vegetables. Beef is expensive and many dishes are made from cheaper meat cuts such as steak and kidney pie, liver and bacon and Black Pudding, a rich dark sausage made from blood and oatmeal. Tea-time, with pots of tea, sandwiches and cakes is another old favourite. Here is how to make some things for tea.

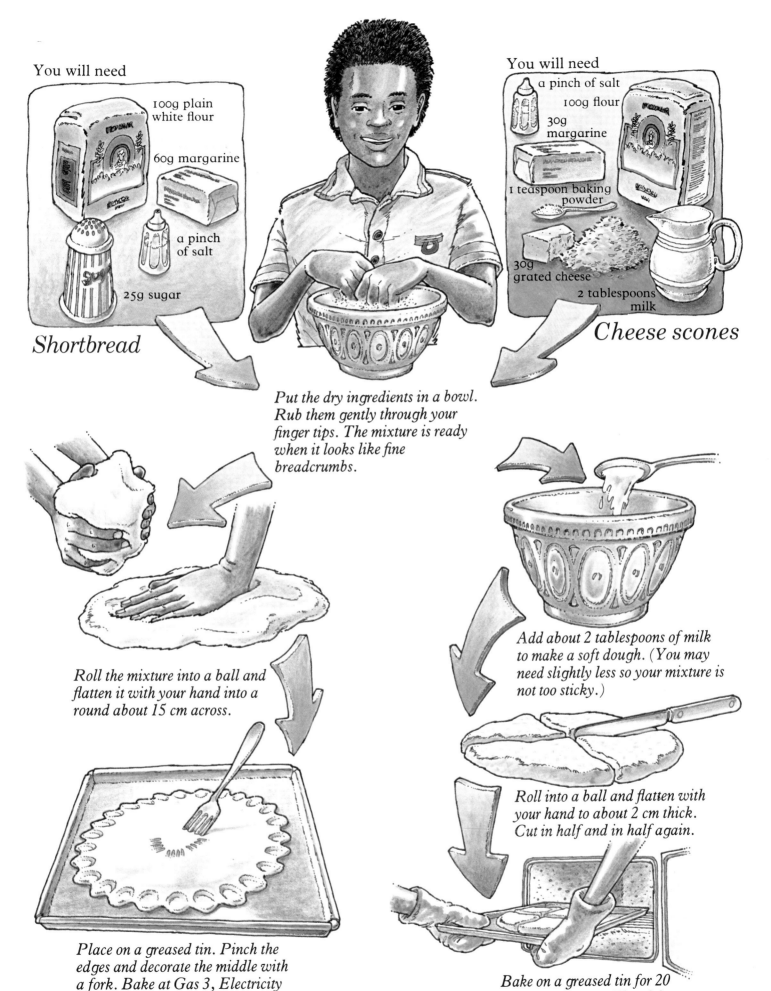

You will need

100g plain white flour

60g margarine

a pinch of salt

25g sugar

Shortbread

You will need

a pinch of salt

100g flour

30g margarine

1 teaspoon baking powder

30g grated cheese

2 tablespoons milk

Cheese scones

Put the dry ingredients in a bowl. Rub them gently through your finger tips. The mixture is ready when it looks like fine breadcrumbs.

Roll the mixture into a ball and flatten it with your hand into a round about 15 cm across.

Add about 2 tablespoons of milk to make a soft dough. (You may need slightly less so your mixture is not too sticky.)

Roll into a ball and flatten with your hand to about 2 cm thick. Cut in half and in half again.

Place on a greased tin. Pinch the edges and decorate the middle with a fork. Bake at Gas 3, Electricity 300°F for 30-40 minutes till golden. Cut in 4 pieces.

Bake on a greased tin for 20 minutes at Gas 7, Electricity 425°F. Eat with butter or cress.

43

Islands around an island

In summer, 61 km of mountain roads in the Isle of Man are closed to run the Tourist Trophy race. It is a very dangerous race but the Manx cat does not seem very interested!

Manx cats come from the Isle of Man, in the Irish Sea. They are born without tails, but no one knows why. Legends say that the cat was a cross between hare and cat. The island is part of Britain but has its own laws, language and coins. Manx people call their home Ellan Vannin.

If you sail north from the Isle of Man, you reach the green islands of Hebrides stretching along the Scottish coast. Many people here speak Gaelic, an old Scottish language. Most people are farmers, but some are weavers too. The woollen cloth which they weave is called Harris Tweed, after one of the islands. Although the tweed is hand-woven (machine-made tweed is not allowed), the weavers make over five million metres a year to send all over the world.

The Shetland Islands are the farthest islands from mainland Britain. Far to the north of Scotland and only 300 km from Norway, they are lashed by North Sea storms. Tough Shetland ponies used to pull trucks down coal mines. They were small enough to work in tunnels only 1.5 m high. Now some children keep them as pets.

After Christmas, Shetlanders celebrate the end of the long winter nights with a festival called Up-Helly-Aa. Men and boys run through the streets with burning torches and tar barrels. At the end of the festival a Viking ship is burned, just like an old Viking funeral when a dead chieftain was burned in his ship. Special songs are sung to mark the funeral of the old year and the birth of the new year.

Index

The dark numbers tell you
where you will find a
picture of the subject

Editorial Manager:
Mary Tapissier

Editor:
John Morton

Picture Research:
Jan Croot

Production:
Rosemary Bishop

Factual Adviser:
Iain Bain, Editor, *The
Geographical Magazine*

Cover Designer:
Camron Design Ltd.

Cover illustrator:
Tony Payne

Teacher Panel:
Eddy de Oro
Anne Serier
Melanie Tanner

Projects:
Barry Milton
Pauline Morton

Eddy de Oro

Illustrator:
Edward Carr

Photographs:
Barnaby's Picture Library   7, 15
Steve Benbow   36/37
Nick Birch   20
British Hovercraft Corporation   8/9
British Tourist Authority   Cover, 10,
38, 41
Camera Press   28
Daily Telegraph   34
England Scene   14/15, 16, 23, 24, 33
Robert Estall   8, 25
Robert Harding   35, 40
Archie Miles   22
Popperfoto   17
Shell   39
Spectrum Colour Library   21, 32
Homer Sykes   45
John Topham   11
Wales Tourist Board   37
Trevor Wood   28/29
Zefa   29

Cover: A Yeoman Warder
from the Tower of London.

A MACDONALD BOOK

First published in Great Britain in 1981
by Macdonald & Co (Publishers) Ltd
London & Sydney

A BPCC plc company

Reprinted 1987

© Macdonald & Co (Publishers) Ltd 1981

All rights reserved

ISBN 0 356 07101 4

Macdonald & Co (Publishers) Ltd
Greater London House
Hampstead Road
London NW1 7QX